The Europeans

The Europeans

David Clarke

Nine
Arches
Press

The Europeans
David Clarke

ISBN: 9781911027690

First published March 2019 by:

Nine Arches Press
Unit 14, Sir Frank Whittle Business Centre,
Great Central Way, Rugby.
CV21 3XH
United Kingdom

www.ninearchespress.com

Printed in the United Kingdom by:
Imprint Digital

Nine Arches Press is supported using public funding by Arts Council England.

Supported using public funding by
**ARTS COUNCIL
ENGLAND**

la naïveté est une condition de la fuite.

Édouard Louis

Contents

Invitation

Meet me in the lobby of the Hotel Europa,
the high lobby shadowed by palms,
where men in uniform stride with stiff
purpose and the pianist gifts us bland jazz.

We'll never spend as many nights
in the Hotel Europa as we would need
to wake just once in all its pristine rooms,
to step lightly onto every balcony.

Let's kiss in the garden of the Hotel Europa,
let's scandalise the dowagers, their hangers-on.
We'll be a mystery to those who meet us,
briefly, at the backgammon table

or in the cocktail hour, when the Hotel Europa
is pearlescent with afternoon light
and the time until dinner is too short for anything
but dozing and minor intrigue.

As soon as we arrive in the Hotel Europa
we long to leave, to find that little place
you once stumbled on – its courtyard walls
rippling with fig trees, its address a fiction.

And yet we cannot fault the service
in the Hotel Europa. Even though it's just after
or just before a war and long-retired
waiters have been pressed back into the ranks

of the white-gloved. Half bent with age,
they're a credit to the Hotel Europa,
younger by decades than most of the guests,
who don't remember their room numbers,

the names of their children,
or even the location of the Hotel Europa
in a land so silent you can hear the blades
of grass turned by the breeze, steam

escaping from the crazed pipework
in the basement of the Hotel Europa,
where the boiler groans from years of obsolescence
and the maître d' is stealing the better wine.

And if we've ever cause to quit the Hotel Europa,
let us not be consumed by recrimination
and regret. Call it a dream,
a happy accident. If you must, a lie.

Letter in March

Old friend, I hope this reaches you. The land's
still yet and sullen as it turns towards
the spring. Dove-grey clouds. Ice expands
in ponds and pipes, while cyan sky rewards
a flash of sun. I hold my breath. These are
the days the people rise. I hear their far-
resounding curse and sigh, as rattled from
electric sleep they wonder what they've won –

a world perhaps, but still it slips away
from them. I walk to town through traffic, sleek
and closed. Wide TVs in shops replay
whatever news we're meant to fear this week.
I watch the outsized heads of talkers talk.
We have to think they're honest now we've bought
their line, but all neat arguments dissolve
to rhetoric. The foolish show resolve,

the barbarous their grit, and every shit
defends the *culture* he does not understand.
Along the morning high street, shops are lit
to show us what we think we want. I stand
before the glass. Crystalled pavement skins
this hunk of ice, the earth, as doubt begins
like hunger, in the guts. Then shoppers come –
I wonder what it is they've really done.

An Exchange

About midday we alighted that muggy coach,
wafted with us packed-lunch air of sweaty hams
and crusty rolls to settle on some verge
beside a modern monument in Essen,
Lichtenstein, or (was it?) Strasbourg-Ouest.

The sky the murk of mushroom soup, the air
a bouillon piqued with too much salt – rich fare
for kids whose land was known for boiling all
it ate. This was the 80s, since you ask,
when chaps in clogs and leather jackets

drilled us through the many conjugations
of *to be*, stroked their strangely sculpted
facial hair, their foreign wives hirsute in places
we didn't dare to guess. *Biology*
or Culture? We could still write that fruitless essay –

just give us rain, an endless afternoon,
the props of that misunderstanding known
once as *exchange* – a plate of soft bread
smeared in offal paste, deep carafes
of wine with plastic caps, cheap cigarettes.

The method we preferred back then was five nights
in a bunk above a snide Johann
or sporty Yves, their dads' impromptu lectures
on the future's dull cascade of peace,
qualified majorities. We took the punctual

buses into reasonable towns, mooched
along the closed arcades, precincts tiled
in abstract forms. We bought ice cream that tasted
of the real thing – a kind of freedom,
mildly strange, like some holiday liqueur

that lurked behind your auntie's sticky sherry,
made from god-knows-what in god-knows-where.
All friends now – that much was true. Our new
careers in smart, sane institutions called,
in deference to all those grandpapas

who came home missing pieces of themselves,
their glass eyes jaundiced by the local brew.
And yet the ante-penultimate evening left us
nothing to say, dried up of ungrammatical
aperçus on heavy metal, the balance of trade.

The final BBQ was underdone,
of course, but then some rebel spiked those beers
that left us gassy on the coach and queasy
lurching from Zeebrugge's quay. And England
loomed, a salty headache in the dawn.

Pale, contrite, we slumped in parents' cars,
forgot all we had learned by Monday's class,
yet dreamed for weeks of that other life.
Forsaking one dull province for another,
we had found ourselves, in fact, transformed.

The Europeans

I saw the Europeans drinking wine under trees.
It was August and their children seemed wise
beyond their years, moving with the dappled light.

Later the Europeans were wearing bright uniforms,
simultaneously grand and preposterous,
their cigarillos discolouring their moustaches.

When the winter came, the Europeans retreated
into forests. People were wolves or wolves
were people. These matters were increasingly unclear.

Every village had good bread, indolent officials,
its own throat-clenching hooch. Occasionally,
its peace was disturbed as love ended in some alleyway.

The Europeans were volatile or taciturn, hearty
or shiftless. Really, you could take your pick.
The only constant was the scrape and shudder of those trams

in the very early morning. In their cities,
the streets were museums. Someone had been shot
heroically on every corner. You could still put your finger

into the bullet holes in the masonry, just as a violin started
up in that apartment over the café. The Europeans
had much to say of poetry and much silence to say it into.

I became convinced they knew something
they would not tell me, but I did not dare
to ask the veterans on the parched square.

To a Black and White Portable Television

Oh, your subtitles, your lovely fuzz of static!
Well past the hour for bed I'd twist your wire antenna,
hold my breath and turn your dial like a safe-cracker,
until those creatures from another world beamed in,

sleek ghosts who stepped all suited, heeled and taloned
from a sexy fog. You knew that glamorous angst
of sin-soaked quays and modernist salons, those anti-
heroes tracing sweat-pricked lips with a brush of thumb.

I had the sound turned low in those provincial nights
to hear my restless mother's tread upon the stair,
rehearsed the argument for culture, my broadened mind.
Oh, your soundtrack of scratchy sax, your jump-

cuts, your sparse credits! How often did I glaze into sleep
as your transmission fizzled out, my dreams a silvered
re-run of those carnal scenes? I'd wake sore-eyed,
then fling back curtains to the morning's monochrome.

The Tarot Reader Shows Me the Hierophant

If memory serves, this card was not dealt out
upon the baize that occupies the opening shot
of Agnès Varda's *Cléo de 5 à 7*.

The intermediary who placed her whispered
bet against our heroine (*elle est perdue!*),
then fobbed her off with platitudes, was that old crone

who turned the cards and gasped. The Hanged Man
jostled Death, a bony joker in the pack.
Such meetings barely count as metaphor.

Hard as it may seem to know our denouement
right from the film's first frame, we may still walk
the streets and try new hats, lithe loafers

now transfigured by those songs we hum.
This was Paris in black and white, of course,
a mirror-decked metropolis, where decades later,

if memory serves, I lurched along the boulevards
in search of liberation, clutching my unthumbed
copy of *The Logic of Sensation*.

No doubt, I'm not the first to search the city
for some sign, to scan its past in celluloid
for that café where I may meet the guide

who's dodged me all my waking life –
even while a surgeon elsewhere rubs
his weary eyes, holds my x-rays to the light.

Museum of Lies

Our unctuous custodian overcharges,
but let that go. Mislabelled vitrines
display the waxen copies of treasures

long since hawked to private hands.
Our system of classification seems
deliberately obscure – harmless

fibs displayed in dusty cases
beside conspiracies, those plots
that gave so many teetering empires

a final nudge. Here's the dead match
of a rumour that lit a pogrom's
blaze, here a perjurer's oath

written in spite. The visitor
may rest a while in a reading room
stuffed with manifestos, slick

brochures for Ponzi schemes, then marvel
at our diorama of hucksters, cultists,
tabloid hacks. Before you leave,

seek out that corner where your own
untruth turns pristine on its plinth,
its every facet catching light.

Rest assured, we keep it safe.

To a Public House

I knew your ash-tray haze of ale, that pitiful booth
for the under-aged, the spinning punctuation of
your fruit machines that trilled, mesmeric in the gloom
between a first necked pint and each man's lonesome trudge

for home. Late it was, then later still. Bleary years
were counted out in wet white rings. Some bloke
who kept a pewter mug behind your bar pegged out
at last. Your jukebox dirged him to his grave.

Tonight the ring-road's rashed with new-builds, flogging
coq au vin and kiddie swings, but still my mouth
is stung with cider, salt. The wind, like memory, assaults
your eaves. Stained carpet sticks to my retreating heels.

Who'll threaten now to split my lip? Who'll stand beside me
to piss in silent prayer? I drink alone in what was once called time.

In the Snug

Little man, you are my grinning birthright,
frog-faced in your better bookie's coat.
You lean against the ale-damp bar of England

and stroke the giggling landlady's chubby hand,
cooing words that stick in bigots' throats.
Little man, you are my chortling birthright –

an army of nothing waits on your command,
as you feed us one more slightly racist joke
and lean across the sticky bar of England

to pinch the fascist barmaid's arse. This land
is randy for the fear that you invoke.
Little man, you are my smirking birthright –

chief soother of our small, yet vicious band
that sneers at Johnny Foreigner, would gloat
to see him dashed against the rocks of England.

In the snug, your fog-horn voice demands
our rapt attention – true and piercing note
that holds us to you, little man. Our birthright
soaks into the blood-warm bar of England.

Let Me Be Very Clear

It's like trying to remove an egg from an omelette, like trading in a three-course meal for a packet of crisps, or for a fruit crumble, or, in fact, for an infinitely large cake. It's like graduating from college with unrealistic expectations, like buying a second home, or agreeing to swap that second home for another house you've never seen, or claiming you've made progress on building that second home when you've only just managed to make yourself a cup of tea. It's like *The Hunger Games*, like *Mad Max*, like *Reservoir Dogs*, like *The Texas Chainsaw Massacre*, like *Love, Actually*. It's like the Blitz, like a military coup, like a punishment beating, like the Treaty of Versailles. It's like Schrödinger's cat, like a wolf without a collar, like a dog that caught the car. And yet it's not like a divorce and not like a walk in the park, although possibly like a walk in the mountains or the moon landing. Maybe it's like a Chocolate Orange, or like the Hotel California, like Roger Federer past his prime, or like Harry leaving One Direction – but definitely not like a golf club, not like refusing to pay for your round in the bar of that golf club, not eating à la carte in the restaurant of that golf club, not like playing a game of golf at that golf club. Really, it's like a frantic bus journey where the passengers are fighting over its speed and direction of travel, where the passengers are required to suck and blow at the same time, where the passengers arrive at a nightclub only to then leave that nightclub and end up in a fight in a kebab shop. It's like jumping off the Titanic, or out of a burning aeroplane without a parachute, or out of a burning aeroplane with a parachute, or out of one burning aeroplane and into another burning aeroplane. It's like a war, like a new kind of freedom, like a jail with the door left open.

The Defence of Bureaucracy

Praise the light at this late hour of afternoon –
the motes it catches in still office air could be
distilled to that grey ink that prints our regulations.

Praise too the lowered heads of all our brothers down
these lino'ed halls, who grade the feathers in your pillow
and classify your waking dreams. We know you curse us

when your case won't fit our latticework of forms,
or when you scrabble at some checkpoint for that scrap
of permit. And who knows better than us how time will slow

in our hot waiting rooms, even as it slips
your grasp like sand or youth. We stood over your birth
with rubber stamps and sealing wax, will write your death

in copperplate in this thin file. The rose you brush
against a lover's cheek is checked by us for greenfly.
The wine you raise in celebration bears our seal.

Sleep safe, O citizen, and do not hear the call
of those slick men who promise freedom from our yoke –
who name us jacks-in-office, apparatchiks, pushers

of pens. They have that glint of buccaneers, the verve
of the frontier. But they will come to poison your well,
then teach your children how to love their sickness.

The Towns

Their prime was built in terraces of brick
that sag now, rooflines buckled under the weight
of years. Somehow, they've forgotten how to sleep,

insomniac in the aisles of the 8-til-late
or slumped in a chicken shop's window. They orbit
estates in patched-up wheels, bear down on morning

like some elusive prey. In market squares
they hold no markets, but rain fills up the space.
They duck into doorways to watch the world dissolve.

Their women are barely speaking, their kids make short
visits. They loiter in alleys to smoke and check
their phones, to hear the echo of heels on cobbles.

Their gables still shoulder faded slogans of commerce,
tattoos to a lover who long since turned away.
They look straight through you when you raise your hand.

When my mother worked in the asylum

its corridors were black rivers.
The mad sailed them like monarchs
in festival barges. The chapel-bell
knelled them like a pious drug.

Tin baths yawned in tall rooms,
lino pooled with signs of struggle.
My mother poured tea as sunlight tumbled
in parkland, aureoled the bald

poisoner as he clung to an oak-stump.
The dementia ward was a staring contest
where God always won, a spell
that made each stranger a never-visiting

child. Singing, somewhere. Or rain, or pills
rattling in plastic cups. The laundry
pressed its shrouds in brittle folds,
weeping forgetful steam. A crocodile

of moon-faced children stumbled across
the lawn, hand in sticky hand.

To a Mellotron

My modern times? That cabaret of neon-
edged sophisticates, all cheap rococo
lit in green and red, its gilt and flock, the floor
love bossa-nova'd across – ecstatic, tight.
Orchestras looped on each magnetic O,
trumpets throbbed in basement air, guttural
reverb's wash of sweaty kitsch. The thrill
of second-city chic and savoir-faire.
Nights handed over like bright coins. I'd hum

my way back home, half-dancing still, by dawn,
eating my bag of chips – a Romeo
late for his shift. Years later, when I'd hear
lush choirs from our kid's room, see shifting scarlet
of his lava lamps curve mystic smoke – O,
then I knew his times would change. Art-school
rockers went progressive, whined and whipped shrill
octaves up and down. And when he went, he
needed nothing, except those gatefolds under his arm.

The Villages

Heat has never suited them –
they squat like disapproving
matrons in threshold shadows
black skirts hitched to the knee.

Truly, it is the rain
they wait on, that does them
instead of talk. Nothing
you have been has been

forgotten, as they shift like sheep
in memory's endless mizzle.
They are a heap of flints
that mark the death of their tribe.

If windows are eyes, theirs
are misted with sly age.
If streets are arteries,
theirs are furred with rust.

They are waiting for you
to blink, to turn off
your engine – widows
in bonnets who outlive

their feckless offspring. At night
their spires are styluses
that scratch a dirge from heaven's
whirling acetate.

To a Stately Home

Drizzle, an oak-lined drive, spectres of sheep.
Electric buggies trundle the infirm
down to that pristine vale you chose to keep

plebeians out of view. Now they form
disorderly queues beneath your portico,
gawp at drapes and family plate, yawn

in front of tarnished oils in gilt that show
your erstwhile owners – tubs of lard on horse
who knew to wield the crop, who let you go

in lieu of tax, but kept a flat, of course,
a tranche of garden, a private gate, the London
house. Tweeded volunteers rehearse

their spiel in dim-lit rooms. You are abandoned
to this leisure world, where those whose kin
would once have scrubbed your marble floors dream on

life *downstairs*. Not for them the sin
of envy. The pleasure's knowing that their betters
had the taste, the loot, the ear of the king

whose pricey chamber remained, despite those letters
of scraping invitation, unused. Autumn
now, the chill end of the season, your shutters

lock in place the dark of a vacant tomb.

The Wreckers' Prayer

Lord, we do not ask for the breaking of ships.
But if You will that breaking, at least permit
us sinners urge it on and glean the spoils.
A gale is up, the parson shakes the pulpit

with his admonitions. He knows what oils
this island's tight machine. Smoke coils
from suddenly extinguished lighthouse fires,
homesteads lour in dark like hunting owls

that twitch for prey. And now our rocks are choirs
that sing of cold and death, the moon conspires
to hide her face in cloud. A boy is sent
to swing a lamp and fool the ship that veers

for shore. The awful sound when hulls are rent
on reefs that run slick black – a screamed ascent
of souls released from flesh by cracking surf.
It barely shakes the hollow firmament.

Lord, You judge not folk that stink of turf-
smoke, that scrape a little life to serve
your power. We pray you look the other way
when live ones crawl up ragged on the wharf

to be dispatched, don't see the sorry quay
that's stained the shade of iodine. Say
we're grit between the stones that grind the world,
say they'd grind without us anyway –

who can blame us then for Fate that hurled
us here upon this isle and deigns to hurl
our booty after. In hard times, let us drop
another needle shining into the well.

The Chicken Catchers

These nights in the van, I'm chasing sleep,
a shrill white fowl that won't hold still,
while ventilators filter the dark
and bleeping cold-trucks grind their gears.

The gang are back at sun-up, smeared
with shit, their faces torn by panicked
claws. Heads slump before they've sucked
the last of post-shift fags. I drive.

Empty fields of England rise
in mist the sun peels back at last
to show a reddish earth. Foxes
amble into scrub by greasy

spoons in lay-bys. I bang my fist
on flaking steel – men stumble, dazed
to breathe the steam from tea
in Styrofoam. I dock it from wages

they've never seen. We are nowhere
now and starved, with so much killing
still to do. We pass a house
with toys in the yard, a woman stands

at the sink and so I think of you.
Every day there's something more
to forgive. I'd call you, love,
but there's another job to do.

To a Telephone Box

The fag-end of that century you made your own –
aptly I inhaled your reek of ash and piss,
then warmed the mouthpiece's patina in my palm,
released a tacky film of strangers' urgency.

Until the pips, I quizzed the helpline volunteers
on all the do's and don'ts, reeling off my night-time
deeds in all the detail they could want. Sequestered
in that half-light cell, I fogged your doll-house panes

and hoped, perhaps, to hear a near and distant voice
that told me all was well. Or then again, I might
have been that lecher in the joke, confessing only
for the thrill of sharing lovely sins. Yet if

the message truly is the medium, I should
have known – as I untwisted your tarnished flex, flicked
the squeaky flap for change, stepped into the rush
of night – that you and I both spoke of our own demise.

The Girl with the Golden Voice

They scratched your sibilance, sweet thing,
from each glass disc they cut for their machine,
erased the air pressed through those two

front teeth, a static charge that pricked
the ears of every sweating engineer
who ever crossed his wires at the GPO.

The suits preferred you prim, precise,
a schoolmarm counting sexless time –
yet still there were those men who claimed

they'd spend three minutes hanging on
the line to catch a breath-trace of that flaw,
imagining you'd whisper them *sweet dreams*

with all the friction of your truer voice.
Left at sixes and sevens by that lovely
hiss, they'd swoon at the third stroke.

England, I loved you

in your verdant years of nostalgia, cloud-harassed
and pungent, a smokestack and chippy in every gulp
of your air. In your talking-shops, your secure
institutions, you'd drink me under every table

you'd carved from the bones of your forests,
bewitch me with your blather of moderate socialism,
the pout of your lovelies in those red-tops
on mornings of damp and desperation.

Now you abandon me to stalk your ghost towers,
shrug me off as a hedge fund jettisons acres
of brownfield, as a state outsources its grief to the lowest
bidder. I only hurt you now so you'll see me again.

Night Porter

I catch you between your room and hers –
if catch is the word. You sheepish in a hotel robe
(that never fits across the gut), me balancing
two trays of room-service dishes, greased and cold.

Downstairs, the last of conference backs are slapped,
the bar-keep slyly checks his watch and yawns.
Fluorescent tubes backstage fizz off, their dust
congealed like beehive wax. Listen now,

my friend, to small-hours silence, never quite
complete. It gives you pause to think before
you make your choice. I've seen it all begin
and end in corridors like these, but never well.

Soon you'll wonder where you put your key,
then shuffle back at 3 a.m., ashamed of what
you did or didn't do. But be my guest.
You didn't see me. I'll swear I never saw you.

Hotel Stationery

Keith from sales is shaking the malfunctioning laser-pointer.
The font's too small on the slides
and Shirley hasn't brought her glasses.

She watches a man who walks across the gravel,
a white blob in his fluffy dressing gown and slippers.
She can smell the pool from here.

Drizzle drenches topiary,
but when the sun comes out for five minutes
everyone takes off their jackets,

wants to walk straight out of here
and never eat another miniature shortbread.
They'll be drowning in emails by the time they get back.

Sales are crumbling across Warwickshire.
Keith refers everyone to the handout.
Alan knows where the fingers should be pointing.

A trolley of sandwiches clatters past the open door.
Nobody's getting a decent signal on their mobile.
A heron or a plastic statue of a heron stands by the pond.

To a Petrol Station

All summer I'd watch those spliffed-up lads lope
across your forecourt's skirt of neon green,
turning out their pockets to buy Rizlas,
ice creams, a fiver's worth of four-star in coppers.

Their thick exhausts brayed into balmy dusk
as I surveyed your chiller cabinet's fare –
week-old samosas, cheap lager and pork pies
adrift in mists of cellophane. A gurgle of coolant

shifted deep inside the machine, electric
motors juddered into insect drone.
Across the fields a combine's alien gale
raised sparks of chaff that caught the rig-lamps' glare.

The trudging habit of centuries had carved
that route you served into fen, while all my forebears
coupled and stayed put in villages
the new had chained in loops of orange light.

At midnight, I'd lock your door and take my place
behind your service hatch to wait for dawn
or those few truckers thundering out to port –
just once, a tear-smeared girl who asked to use the phone.

I hear you're boarded up these days and thistles
crack your concrete. Now I speed down distant roads
and guess there's no one left to count the change.

For the Traveller

Choose the time of your departure with care –
most any hour will do. Along your road
the brazen foxes will trot for home, a muffled
workman will flick his butt into the hedge.
Your pack will make an ache that's soon a part of you.

*

You'll shiver with the dew in grass at junctions,
air that's sweet from diesel and damp. You'll slide
into a stranger's car, the radio's news
of all you'll leave behind, and watch the A-road's
raptors skim the darkening verge for blood and fur.

*

The sea rears up. You'll find you have to say
its name. You'll quickly learn the argot of ports –
salt on metal, a café's bilious fry
that clings to breeze. You'll speak it with a tremor
in the morning's throat, your vision ozone-blurred.

*

Each time you look, your passport photo will seem
less like you. Your hand will move to those small
bills you've hidden away, a loser's tell.
But then the ocean will thump your rusted hull,
a sorry engine will quake till it becomes your heart.

*

Be prepared for days of cheese and bread,
beer that's passed in bottles around a carriage
after dawn. The orange fabric of worn
seats will leave its pattern on your cheek.
Suddenly, like strangers' laughter, there'll be heat.

*

You'll unpeel yourself, your few clothes stowed
in musty disarray. You'll smell your body –
a scent the sun lifts from you as you walk.
That first town will have its creamy square,
the gravel fresh as seashells where the sprinklers twirl.

*

Shawled women will cross your path at noonday,
while husbands lean to smoke and spit in shade.
A row of iron lampposts will flake green
along a promenade that's built to cusp
the lake-shore's curve. Mountains will seem blue, then red.

*

The room you'll rent, its shutters cracked with light –
you'll take it for the start of everything.
You'll have one book, half-read, to dream an end to
every night. The concierge will claim
there was a famous poet here, who left or died.

*

Sometimes you'll want to use their words – the ones
for that black wine you can't afford, those little
balls of dough they toss in shallow fat.
But soon the call of borders will take your mind –
you'll sit each day to watch that yellow bus depart.

*

You'll study maps of the frontier, its demarcation
etched in pink. You'll reckon it's a week
on foot, one raw thumb thrust into the road.
You'll know this means you're never going home.
From there on in, my friend, you will be on your own.

Auden at Kirchstetten

All morning, his difficult love kept itself to the kitchen,
sweating, as always, to make its comfort terrible.
If a family habit of property had survived
his makeshift years, he refused to become responsible –
somehow he contrived to never fully arrive,
if only for the sake of that necessary tension.

The irregular man must keep regular hours, stand
at intervals to gaze from the green balcony
into the garden's argument, deciding again
not to write of corpses of ash, humanity's
clean causes calling for blood. Occasional rain
would shake the cornflowers, cool his outstretched hand.

He did want not to make the fissured world whole
in his song about the gorgeous luck of being alive.
Whatever was asked of him, he'd find a way to refuse,
to make light – most frivolous when at his most grave.
The work became his witness to all he planned to lose,
speaking in grand reticence of the hope of the soul.

Each day, around eleven, he shuffled the neat track,
raised a hand in greeting to the druggist, the priest.
In the bar, a glass of lager beer, soft bread.
Lion-headed he sucked at his last few teeth
and let what might be sayable remain unsaid.
His many exiles had become a turning back.

Laudatio

Whose pale hands are those in all his dreams,
laid lifeless on a counterpane?

His mother gone too early or his brother
dragged out white and weedy from the pond?

No matter – we guess some such affair
was at the start of all those paintings, speeches,

string quartets that stitch the cloth of light
where it was torn that day by evil.

He knows what we all know, but do not know –
we walk on earth that hardly bears our tread,

our neighbour is a murderer in waiting,
the metaphors we use for dread

(weather, wolves and birds, a hole in the ground)
are nothing next to what he saw and cannot

now unsee. He comes to middling towns
like ours to accept the savings bank prize,

to give one of his lectures on the reach
of culture, complete with kind remarks

about our finely buttressed church.
Here is a giant civic key, here

a box of our famous cakes. We are relieved
to see him drive alone back into the night.

To a Small Audience

What brings you here, these fallow nights,
to this cold room above a pub?
Don't answer that. Just try to press
some comfort from your awkward seat,

your eyelids heavy with the dregs
of that last pint. My warm-up pops
the mic with earnest speech. He stands
too close, in art as so much else.

I watch you grimly wait for this
to end, to be at last released,
and know you are not here for me.
I won't or can't object to that.

Still, I've got you now, with twenty
minutes on the clock and little
mercy to spare. Buckle up.
This won't be fun for any of us.

What I need to conjure here
is only made from my short breath.
Imagine a man who wrestles his shadow –
better, a shadow wrestling

with its man. Words and flesh
will almost meet, though neither lose
their strangeness. When this is done,
I guarantee you'll not be changed –

although the air may shift in ways
that I can't seem to name.

Linguaphone

If you let the new words stick
like pavement gum in the tread of your brain,
the signifier's plump thumb will smear
the signified's mascara. Strain

those gobstopper vowels inside your cheek
to fabricate for the world a dumb-tongued
double, a gap-toothed, stumbly twin.
Now you are asking the way to the station,

now you order a sandwich, a coke.
Like wearing a stranger's dashing hat,
embarking in error a branch-line train,
the shifting landscape's parallax

composed of sounds that are not sense,
becoming speech in the passengers' babble.
You smoke by the window and learn by rote
what's strictly correct, yet sweetly improbable.

To a Photo Booth

You'd leave me blind, blurred
by that first flash. The world
dissolved in after-flare
that burst on my retina's screen.

The second exposure streamed
with snot and tears. You spat
me out to dry beside
my red-faced, grieving twin,

the mugshot of a petty
crook who'd stumbled into
the arms of the law.
I disowned him then,

snipped my sad unlikeness
from the ones half-good
for railcards, permits, gummed
to index cards by Personnel.

My drawers grew full of all
your rejects, curled ghosts
who wept in envelopes unseen.
One day, I guessed, I'd have

some use for sorrow's secret face.

Lingua franca

This vault of glass and steel's a lung,
the station breathes us in and out
where schoolkids come to mill about
and pigeons find a patch of sun

to preen their filthy plumes. My mother
tongue's commercial here, the voodoo
spell of lifestyle choice, those untrue
worlds of poster girls who bother

with their *Wellness* creams, relax
in steaming baths of *natural foam*.
Then the cheery Serb who runs
the kiosk for wurst and booze asks

in broken English where I'm from.
My forebears once re-named the world,
turned it pink as fresh-cut veal.
Their empire's accents are still strong

in all our speech, an odd kind of
ventriloquism. But here's a pleading
boy with war-blank eyes, needing
change in his cup. They shoo him off,

this pensioned German pair, intone
a phrase they somehow must recall
from lessons of their own post-war –
Go home!, they say, *Go home!*

The Clock

We reached the Sultanate at night from the sea,
rocked to the beach in our launch, the clock intact
in its crate. Sun slipped through slats,
glanced flashes of pink, motion of cogs.

As Schmidt and Van Deusel heaved on the oars,
I pondered this freight, selected by the Prince
himself, his white-gloved fingers caressing its etched
illustration. He'd smiled at nymphs all a-dance

around that temple to art and science, a time-piece
like a miniature folly, wafted by gauzes
that clung to the breasts of its fleshy denizens.
Its clicks were the soporific pulse of progress,

its chimes the quickening laugh of a silver girl.
No offering was better designed to prick
the Mohammedan's envy of our advances,
his admiration for our race. The investment

of nigh-on one hundred Talers was surely sound,
but not the only cost. The forging of sea-ways,
the charting of lands we had crossed by mule, on foot –
all this we could count as success. And still

I could not forget the loss to the crew of limbs,
lopped off by our saw-bones, those loosening
headfuls of teeth, the madness of young Lefebvre.
Now, at the carved teak gates of the Sultan's compound,

bearers strained beneath the burden. A wizened
muezzin bade us follow him through a maze
of pot-palms, wind chimes, blue-tiled fountains.
My fellows jemmied a single creaking plank.

The old man peered, gasped, stood back –
then ushered us out, muttering thanks.
The Sultan was weary and could not receive us.
And yet, as we retreated, I'd swear on the Scriptures

I glimpsed him – a rotund potentate reclined
in his orangery, lost among vellum-bound volumes.
He toyed with arcane instruments
in the patterned shadows of an ornate screen.

The Amber Room

I am a solider, so cannot find the words
to conjure for you now that air or light.
Let us say that it was radiance.

By this I mean, I felt as if I entered
childhood summers refined into the surface
of a pool, whose glare bright insects skimmed.

From photographs, you see that it was kitsch.
I myself prefer a modern line.
Even so, those artisans had made

another world of honey, citrus, wax.
An antechamber of God's mind. And yet,
inside, all sound was sharp, my bones more brittle

in their flesh. It was unease. The city
shook, fractured street by street. We had
so little time, no tools but breaking-irons

and hammers, crates and straw. I gave my youth
to shape this continent anew, but now
it smashed to sickly grit beneath my boots.

And still I enter that room each restless night
to find it is a prison much like this.
My confession, I hope, may mitigate.

Sugar Town

Tacky to the touch
it leaves its residue
on all our days, hardens
to translucent glaze
on skin trade's bitter facts.

Such sweetness is a kind
of tact, a sugar tax
that's levied on discretion,
as rough plantation cane's
refined to sickly stucco.

The town museum's rammed
with china cups, moulds
for shape and jelly fruits –
the gubbins that got children
hooked on candy highs.

Beneath the cinder-toffee
streets molasses seeps,
a river black and hot
as distant toil. Glucose
peaks in blood, a coma

like a blessèd sleep,
while holes are bored in teeth
that whistle in the morning
wind. The poison's still
concealed in sugar cubes

on outstretched tongues.

To an Airmail Letter

Did someone choose your blue, perhaps, to match
translucences of sky that spanned the veld?
They milled you slight as mountain-station air.
In any case, you caught those gossamers
of platitude that bulged our history's mailsacks,
propellered into stodgy English cloud.

Maybe twice a year you would surprise
your addressees with that cerulean wash,
a break between the grey. You'd bring them news
of dogs and crops, buck-shot fired across
the wire at restive natives, who skulked at dusk
in revolution's patched fatigues.

Or from Hong Kong you'd send for hope,
worn paper-thin. Those sweat-necked men,
who forced their script into your brittle skin,
begged another thousand from back home
to seal the deal. A spare sheet served as blotter
for spilled gin. You languish in some attic

now, bundled into trunks that caught
the last ship out. You taught us to be spies –
your leaves were tissue-wrap for family secrets,
each humdrum note a palimpsest of true desire.
It ran right through you like a water-mark.
We never thought to hold you to the light.

The Numbers Stations

Discreetly he descends the stair
in Bucharest or Sevastapol,
with secrets pressed beneath his tongue
to brave the howl of Europe's night.

Divided heavens are turning slow
as numbers stations chant their codes.
Gagarin Street's a lightless flume
where Ladas swing their beams to catch

the grizzled guards who doze at their posts,
then roll in neutral down to a lake
and make the drop before dawn breaks.
I hear it too, that litany,

a hot transistor pressed to my ear.
Beneath the sheets of suburbia's calm
the double-agent of desire
betrays my body's strange terrain.

The shortwave tunes me to that place
where cold bureaucracies of lies,
hard cash and expeditious sex
intone enchanted shibboleths.

Counting out its mysteries
this voice implies some dirty trick,
which, mastered, could unlock the world.
It hisses brightly in my mind.

The Natives

They have a particular way to imagine the soul –
witness their intricate death-masks. Do not ask
which creature they milk to sour this pungent tonic
we cannot even pronounce. Like us, they have furious

dances, the costumes passed from matron to maid –
girls swing from each other's studded belts,
lads lean and twirl their straggling beard-hairs.
The goods they fashion turn to trinkets

in our hands. Their gods become our gnashing
phantoms, scourging sleep. And when we bend
to enter fusty taverns, their looks remind us
that we are no-one at all.

On Choosing a Piano

They sold two kinds – lacquered caskets,
lids propped to display the guts,
then those varnished bourgeois sideboards,
all candleholders and inlaid posies.

The owner called a flunky in greasy
tails and brilliantine from the back
to coax a minuet from his priciest
upright, to grin as I thumbed fresh bills.

They sent a donkey cart, a haulier's
young apprentice, who heaved on tackle,
swung that felt-wrapped case of silence
over my balcony, eyed me

sidelong as I proffered lemonade.
His shirt clung. A crowd dispersed
like crows across the white piazza.
I took my penny primer

that explained the keys, contorted
my hand to shape that virgin chord.
The warm air's tremor drained into
my fingertips – and so I pressed

again, again, to ring all afternoon
inside myself. My body made
a maple box that zinged with wires.
The town was still till evensong,

when all its bells swung into this
first music I'd invented. And yet,
I'd never know that country.
By morning, I'd packed my bags to leave.

Letter to George Gordon Byron

Dear G, I think you may forgive my cheek
    as I address you without that lordly title
and shake you rudely from your embalmed sleep.
    I hear you're well preserved, so the fright will
not do too much harm, I hope. We keep
    on coming back to you, we scribblers, entitle
ourselves to your estate of rhyme. My weak
effort's more a sideways way to speak

of troubles you would no doubt recognise.
    A puffed-up England sneers again at all
that's foreign, toffs are cheered by plebs they despise.
    Schemers promise the mob to 'send them all
back', but smirk as they betray. Each vies
    to unseat pale Mrs May. Her downfall
will seem small to you, yet who recalls
your Castlereagh? In short, the scene appals.

And I've not even mentioned our free press,
    the voice of England's bigotry and smuggery.
You'd not fare too well with them today, I'd guess.
    (They've not lost their old distaste for buggery.)
They've hate for all the joy that they repress
    and screeching you'd dismiss as verbal thuggery.
Wits like you are monstered for daring to be
an offence to journos' propriety.

And still you'd find that freedom's not a cause
    for which the English like to stir their bones.
They flog their bombs to those who'll pay, of course,
    then put high fences right around their homes,
vote to make a fortress of the borders.
    This land loves fear, yet reckons that the groans
of the oppressed are just put on, disowns
the fate of its own far-off conflict zones.

Agreed – so far my song's not very fetching.
   Verse should be subtle to reveal its truth.
This is just a complex form of kvetsching,
   ineptly done (that last rhyme is the proof).
What's more, these stanzas are proving rather vexing.
   You'd knock out endless cantos in your youth.
Some critics claimed your manner was perplexing,
but you had talent – and looks, which are the main thing.

Nobody reads you now, it's sad to relay,
   save undergrads who slog through their exams.
One writes, 'he was a big noise in his day.
   When he croaked he still had many plans –
to liberate the Greeks and do away
   with foreign despots. Such inspired demands
suit our own age. What would he likely say
to Brexit? If he were still alive today

he'd cheer, despite extreme old age.' This student's
   Young Conservative or worse – a bater
of his right-on profs, for sure. Imprudent
   he may seem to pen such guff, yet cater
to all views his teachers must. Impudent
   rascals who earn Thirds cry foul and later
sue for breach of contract. Their alma mater
would prefer them to become donators.

That student has a point, I must admit,
   on your beloved Greece. You'd weep to see
it coshed by men in suits who seem legit,
   but have a banker's taste for liberty,
i.e. not much of one. And what won't fit
   the markets' needs is ripe for pillory –
jobless Greeks are supernumerary,
just like quaint notions of equality.

Right-thinking folk will overlook these faults
    of European peace. Besides, they travel
widely and love Paris well. Assaults
    upon their right to shop in Rome, then marvel
idly at St Peter's gilded vaults,
    are not well received. They curse the rabble
who queered their cushy pitch, but what revolts
them most is that the revolting dared to revolt.

And who can blame them? After all, they've got
    those tabloid-reading troglodytes to thank
that their kids will miss out on that spot
    with the Commission or (better) Deutsche Bank.
Truly, you can't envy them their lot –
    the most their darlings can hope for now's a think-tank
or a civil service job. The rank
injustice of it all is clear. I drank,

dear G, a toast to you the other day.
    Can you guess, deep in your tomb, the cause?
The date of your arrival at Missolonghi,
    in 1824. I've seen those shores
where you alighted to acclaim, away
    from home yet finding home in others' wars.
I'm too much a coward to choose your way,
but let my poem mark that anniversary.

Station to Station

Zoologischer Garten

The dawn comes pre-soundtracked –
shimmers of Moog, the plosive tick
of a drum machine. Pigeons are analogue,
scatter across the opening pan of this travelogue.

Nottingham Central

Tea too hot to drink in cups too hot
to hold. There's no melt to this frost.
Midlands murk. We're not making a scene.
You have one case. You're taking everything.

Milano Centrale

My eyes marble, my head a restless vault.
Noise never ends, trains never arrive. Stop
me if you've heard this one before. History
throws down the mise-en-scène of my small misery.

King's Cross

Nostalgia's the last thing we need.
This used to be drunks, boys offering you weed.
We're too old for the night now anyway.
Shut up and suck the froth from your latte.

Antwerpen-Centraal

More like a palace, ducal at the very least.
The tannoy has no news of our release
from the quaintness of industrial action,
or, failing that, from the quaintness of this nation.

Leeds Central

I saw that bloke from that band you liked.
The jacket no longer leather, the hair no longer spiked.
These concourses are the best place to learn
there's no such thing as the eternal return.

Apparition

I've heard it told like this. A teacher scolded
boys who raised the alarm, until he caught
a whitish glimpse of haunch beyond the yard.

An ugly machine of bones, draped in piss-stained
carpet, a lumber so close to falling it stung
the heart. The only man in town who owned

a rifle took aim, then let his weapon fall.
The creature collapsed against a mini-mart's steps,
as people came from air-conditioned houses.

They crouched on tarmac to offer tins of meat,
someone even suggested frozen fish.
It didn't seem to recognise the food.

Experts charted oceans its paws had parted,
plotted its track across the forests' tinder.
The mighty head lolled in an Arctic dream.

Some say it wanted nothing we possessed,
had long since taken leave of sorrow.
We didn't know that ours had just begun.

Land of Rain

I found this app that played me rain –
its scattershot on Nissen huts,
its pat-a-cake on low-grown shrubs.

Then cannonades from fractured downpipes,
a picnic-drowning deluge, drizzle
melting into cloud on fell.

I searched for hapless Sunday childhood
rain, scrolled through cold applause
that greets the thunder's show –

but only in my exile's sleep
did I retrieve my sodden place,
my land of rain.

The Vision of Albion

Weighing this half-brick in my hand,
still sucking seeds between my teeth,
I took the road to the river bank,
where poplars lay their lick of shade,
and stretched my bones on tawny grass.

Heat that came and went like song,
a creeping dampness from the ground –
this country never warms you through,
or not for long, I said to myself as sirens
streaked the breeze. Order fails,

so let the chaos have its chance –
let's give ourselves to this cold rage
that wakes us just before the dawn
to yank devices from their wires
and bathe our faces in strange light.

Our sleep is short and shallow,
makes us sicker still. My watch was cracked,
the long hand jittered, out of time,
and down the valley some great force
was shouldering still, the glacier's ghost.

My knuckles scuffed, my vision off.
The riot of memory fading out,
its last few stragglers shuffling home
as sun dipped into managed fields,
their hedgerows twitched with a charge

of voles and birds, buds unclasping
on the beam. The world was full
of something all about its end,
the new held for a moment like a breath –
I held my own and stared into

the vault of night, to watch a satellite
skim past, its little pulse of light,
before I sloped back down a lane,
to try the door of that squat church.
It rattled like a box of nails,

a pit of flints and arrowheads,
an empty grave. Birds burst up.
I heard a car that throbbed with bass,
a pale illumination spun
into the land I made to leave.

A ring-road glanced a suburb's flank,
my limbs were heavy with themselves.
Forgive whatever now you think
I've left undone. Have mercy
for the merciless, save comfort

for this awkward age. The country's
lonely with itself and howls
for something, like a dog gone old
in the head. A raw demand,
it pulls and pulls against its chain.

Notes and Acknowledgements

The quotation from Édouard Louis is taken from his novel *Histoire de La Violence* (Paris: Éditions du Seuil, 2017).

'Let Me Be Very Clear' is a collage of similes that have been used by politicians and journalists attempting to describe the process of the United Kingdom exiting the European Union.

'To a Mellotron': the Mellotron was first manufactured in Birmingham in 1963. An early form of sampler, it was a keyboard instrument that played pre-recorded sounds on loops of magnetic tape. In the 1970s it became popular with progressive rock bands.

Some details in 'The Wreckers' Prayer' were inspired by Kevin Crossley-Holland's *Pieces of Land: Journeys to Eight Islands* (Victor Gollancz, 1972).

The starting-point for 'England, I Loved You' was Sara Ahmed's *The Cultural Politics of Emotion* (Edinburgh University Press, 2004).

'Auden at Kirchstetten' draws on details from *Auden* by Richard Davenport-Hines (Heinemann, 1995) and on some formal aspects of Auden's own poem 'Voltaire at Ferney' in *Collected Shorter Poems 1927–1957* (Faber and Faber, 1966).

'The Amber Room' refers to a room decorated with some 6 tonnes of carved amber that was gifted to Peter the Great by the Prussian King Frederick William I in the early 18th century. The room was looted from St Petersburg by German forces during the Second World War and subsequently disappeared.

'The Numbers Stations' were short-wave radio broadcasts during the Cold War, which repeated sequences of numbers believed to have transmitted messages to intelligence operatives in the field. This poem is dedicated to Eley Furrell.

'Letter to George Gordon Byron' owes a debt to Fiona MacCarthy's *Byron: Life and Legend* (Faber and Faber, 2003) and, of course, to W.H. Auden's 'Letter to Lord Byron' in *Collected Longer Poems* (Faber and Faber, 1968).

Some of these poems appeared in the following publications: 'Invitation' in *Magma*; 'When My Mother Worked in the Asylum', 'The Chicken Catchers' and 'To a Telephone Box' in *Bare Fiction*; 'In the Snug' in *New Boots and Pantisocracies*, edited by W.N. Herbert and Andy Jackson (Smokestack Books, 2016); 'To a Mellotron' in *This Is Not Your Final Form: Poems About Birmingham*, edited by Richard O'Brien and Emma Wright (The Emma Press, 2016); 'The Natives' and 'Linguaphone' in *Poetry Salzburg Review*; 'Land of Rain' in *Envoi*; 'Auden at Kirchstetten' in *Strix*. I am grateful to the editors and publishers concerned.

'Night Porter' and 'Hotel Stationary' were written as the result of a residency in 2016 at Billesley Manor Hotel near Stratford, supported by Stratford-upon-Avon Poetry Festival, the Shakespeare Birthplace Trust and Arts Council England. 'The Girl with the Golden Voice' was originally written for the Ledbury 2017 edition of S. J. Fowler's 'Camarade' project.

I am indebted to Jane Commane of Nine Arches Press for her skill as an editor and her faith in these poems. I am also grateful for the support and advice of many friends in poetry, including Alison Brackenbury, Chaucer Cameron, Helen Dewbery, Angela France, Adam Horovitz, Nina Lewis, Michael Loveday, Philip Rush, Anna Saunders and the rest of the team at Cheltenham Poetry Festival, and (above all) Jennie Farley. Finally, none of this would happen without Malcolm Allison.